Yolanda Bravo Saldaña

W9-BIQ-835

MEXICO CITY

HISTORY · ART · MONUMENTS

200 Colour illustrations

MONCLEM
EDICIONES

BONECHI

CONTENTS

INTRODUCTION

Mexico City has been seen in many different ways throughout time. In the pre-Hispanic period it was "the Navel of the Moon", while in 1554 the humanist Francisco Cervantes de Salazar wrote that a walk through its streets "brings joy to the soul and delights the eye". In the early 17th century the poet Bernardo de Balbuena qualified it as "the finest flower of all cities, the glory of the West". The chronicler Juan de Viera was amazed by its baroque buildings and splendid cathedral in the 18th century. In the 19th century it was recognized as "The City of Palaces" and in our days the writer Carlos Fuentes has christened it "The most transparent region of the air".

But Mexico City is more than just fine-sounding phrases: the apparent silence of a street, a square, a monument, a church or a park cloaks the voice of the centuries; it is a vast data bank, ready to give up its secrets to those who care to tap into it. This, the nerve center of the country, has been a densely populated area ever since its beginnings. Its pivotal role in comparison to the other cities of the country is reflected in the annals of the nation - from the splendor of Great Tenochtitlan to most recent events.

Chronologically, Mexico City's most important historical periods are as follows. From 1325 to 1521, when the Aztec capital was founded, took shape, expanded and then declined. This last date saw the beginning of one of the great American epics: the struggle between the Spanish and the Aztecs who finally surrendered to the conquistador Hernán Cortés. After the fall of pre-Hispanic civilization the territory was made a viceroyalty that lasted from 1535 to 1821, the year when criollo society liberated itself from Spain. In 1864 Maximilian of Hapsburg arrived with his wife Charlotte (Carlota) to be emperor and ruled through a political illusion that was to end in 1867 with his execution by firing squad and the establishment of a Republic with Benito Juárex as its president. A few years later one of the most controversial figures in Mexican history rose to power: Porfirio Díaz, who governed the country for thirty years. A third war broke out in 1910, this time against the Díaz dictatorship - the Mexican Revolution - ending in 1921. In this year the capital and the rest of the country struck out on the road toward modernization, internationalization and the realization of what it was to be Mexican.

In the 1950's Mexico City, the core of the nation's history, began to grow not only spiritually but also spatially. Wide avenues were driven through it, rivers were capped and the number of motor vehicles grew at an amazing rate, to the extent that nowadays there are more than 3.5 million in the metropolitan area.

This city has been the setting for the most important moments in Mexico's history and is the home of its most dazzling monuments. Any Mexican who lives in it is a synthesis of the past, a fusion of Aztecs, criollos, and the Independence-seeking and Revolutionary spirits of the 19th and 20th centuries.

According to calculations Mexico City with its 16 precincts and associated boroughs will possibly still be the largest city in the world in the year 2000, with 25 million inhabitants living in an area of 1,700 sq. km. - the famous urban sprawl.

At present the city has a population of almost 20 million. These are people proud of its past because all its buildings, whether of adobe, volcanic rock, limestone, marble, iron, wood, aluminum, concrete or glass remind them every day that this metropolis where they live has been the center of the nation for over 650 years.

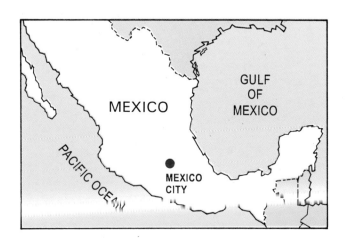

colhuacan. pueblo. tenayucan. pueblo.

Left. The first plate of the Mendocino Codex shows the original layout of Mexico-Tenochtitlan. In the center is the figure of the Aztec tutelary god, Huitzilopochtli, in the shape of an eagle.

One of the most important Nahuatl codices, the Tira de la Peregrinación, mentions that the people who settled in Mexico-Tenochtitlan came from a place called Aztlán.

MEXICO-TENOCHTITLAN

Mexico City lies in a great basin formed by complex volcanic activity and tectonic movements dating back 50 million years, while man first arrived in this region known as the Central Plateau 25 thousand years ago. But it is only since the 14th century until our own days that these lands have seen not only one but several urban conglomerates take shape, grow, decline and then rise again - like a Phoenix - under the same name.

The first inhabitants of this region of five lakes were nomad hunters, but toward 100 B.C. the civilization was influenced by the great culture of the Olmecs. Archaeological remains show that this was when important communities grew up in Zacatenco, El Arbolillo, Cuicuilco and Teotihuacan.

The most important building stage of Cuicuilco was in the 5th century B.C. Its circular pyramid, an enigma which still stands in the south of the city, measures over 120 meters in diameter and is 20 meters high with a clay and stone core. When Cuicuilco disappeared under the lava spewed out by the *Xitle* volcano the second city of the region, Teotihuacan, rose to power. This city, which saw its heyday in the 2nd century A.D. was abandoned after the 8th century and is now one of Mexico's most important archaeological sites both for its architecture and its urban design.

Many centuries had to go by before a culture settled on this territory that could create a city able to hold sway over neighboring communities. In the 14th century a group from the north, Aztlán to be exact, founded the greatest religious, political, military and commercial center in pre-Hispanic America. Documents such as the *Tira de la peregrinación* relate that after long wanderings the Aztecs or Mexica arrived on an island in Lake Texcoco in 1325. Its name was *Metzlipan* (a Nahuatl word meaning "the navel of the moon"). This region belonged to the Tepanecas, and it was here that the Aztecs saw their god

The splendor of Mexico-Tenochtitlan as seen by the great Mexican muralist Diego Rivera, who depicted most of Mexico's four centuries of history on the walls of the National Palace.

Huitzilopochtli, changed into an eagle, who showed them where they had to found his city and raise a temple to him.

The Aztecs followed the divine orders of their tutelary god and after founding the city divided it into four sections with the place where the legendary bird appeared as its center. The city was built around this central point occupied by the great pyramid and was organized from it. The temple was a sacred place for the Aztecs, the heart of their city and the core of their vision of the universe; it was an earthly reproduction of the image they had of a universe divided into four quarters. In Tenochtitlan these religious parts became four large districts: Cuepopan, Atzacoalco, Zoquipan and Moyotlán which each had their communal area with a temple, school, palace and a square in some cases.

Since the island was very small, the Aztecs created "floating" fields *(chinampas)*, built up of stones and mud and anchored by a system of piles to make them more stable.

These were very important in Aztec food production, and at the same time huts were built on them. As the years went by this technique helped to weave the great city together. These plots of land were so fertile that they are now considered to be one of the most efficient systems of intensive agriculture ever devised in pre-industrial times.

At first, buildings were of simple materials such as reeds and mud, and people simply lived off what the lake provided. In the course of time of less perishable materials were used for buildings, including the first great temple to the Sun god which, following the sun's course, was oriented east to west. The palaces of the most important lords were built around the ceremonial area.

From 1325 to 1428 Tenochtitlan - so named in honor of the god *Tenoch* - remained under Tepaneca rule. The first governor of the Aztecs was Acamapichtli, but it was under Itzcóatl that they succeeded in dominating the enemy territories of Azcapotzalco, Xochimilco and Coyoacán, thanks to a Triple Alliance with Texcoco and

The Florence Codex, produced by Indians under the supervision of Fray Bernardo de Sahagún, relates some aspects of everyday life among the Aztecs. On the left, a child is learning to read, while on the right a featherwork artist is at his difficult task.

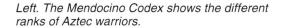

Left. The Mendocino Codex shows the different ranks of Aztec warriors.

The Florence Codex also shows how the ancient Aztecs hunted birds on the shores of the lakes surrounding Tenochtitlan.

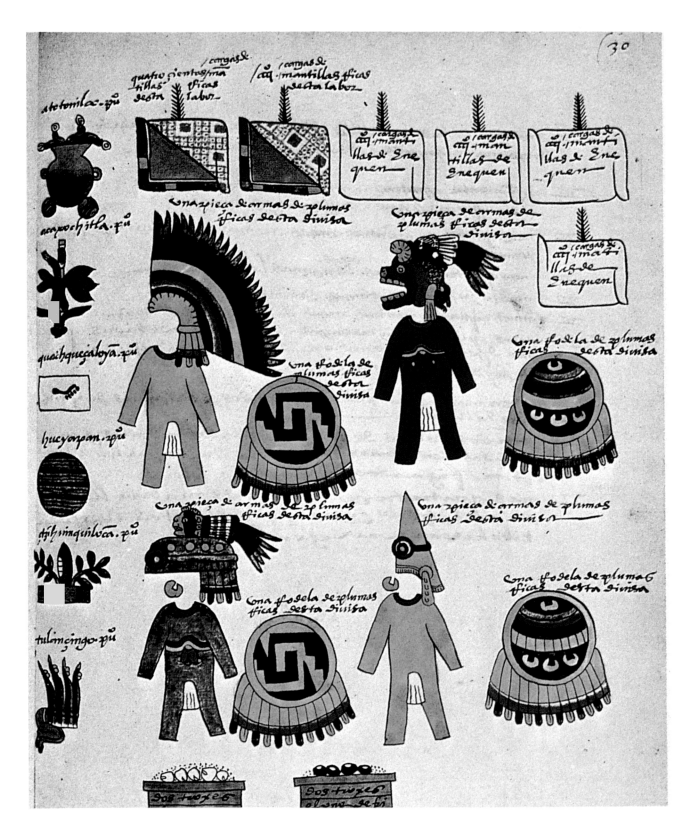

The Mendocino Codex lists the tributes that the various towns dominated by the Aztecs had to deliver. This plate shows bunches of precious feathers, bags of cochineal to make dye, jade beads and other products.

Following old diagrams the architect Ignacio Marquina drew this view of the Great Temple of Tenochtitlan.

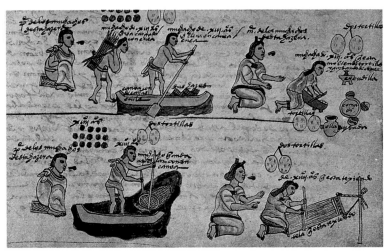

The Mendocino Codex shows how Aztec youngsters were educated: mothers taught their daughters how to cook and weave, while fathers explained fishing and trading to their sons.

Tacuba. These conquests ensured the growth of Tenochtitlan and at the same time secured more productive land. The *Teocalli* or Great Temple, dedicated to both *Huitzilopochtli* and *Tláloc*, was expanded and its ornamentation made richer; its courtyards were laid out and a large stone wall known as the *coatenantli* or "wall of serpents" similar to the one on the archaeological site of Tenayuca was built. Since they now ruled the lake shores the Aztecs designed a complex system of ditches, dikes, causeways and aqueducts, thus gaining control of all the valley's water. More *chinampas* were created and water

was retained and regulated with a system of locks.

Aztec temple bases were generally topped by a platform, and their sloping sides were interrupted by terraces, while a wide steep staircase flanked by ramps led up to the summit. They were surrounded by lush gardens, spacious squares and white buildings. Whenever a new ruler took office, the Great Temple was altered.

The great building period of Tenochtitlan was initiated by Moctezuma I, who decreed several sanitary improvements for his people. He built an aqueduct running from the springs of Chapultepec that supplied plentiful drink-

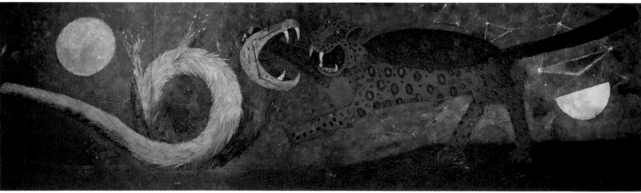

Above. The National Museum of Anthropology illustrates the history of pre-Hispanic peoples through displays of the works of art and objects they produced. The upper floor is devoted to the ethnography of Mexico.

Below. The Oaxacan artist Rufino Tamayo painted the entrance hall of the National Museum of Anthropology with his vision of Day and Night, a work full of pre-Hispanic symbolism.

Above right. Tláloc, the god of Rain and Lightning. This 4.5-meter-tall monolith greets the hundreds of people who visit the National Museum of Anthropology every day.

Below right. The Anthropology Museum has this reconstruction of the Great Temple, the sacred area of the Aztec capital, where the size of the ceremonial complex can be appreciated.

MUSEO NACIONAL DE ANTROPOLOGIA

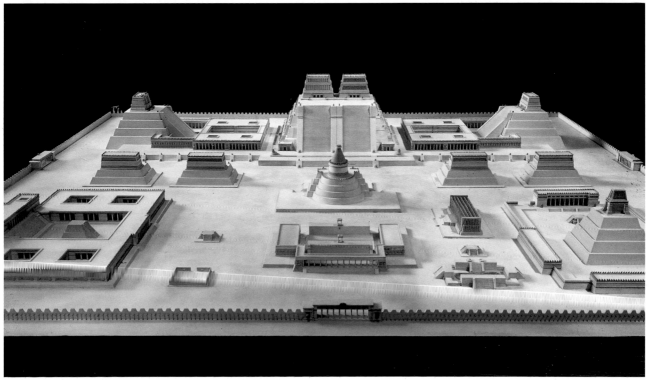

Model of Tlatelolco market, the largest and most important one on the Central Plateau, in the National Museum of Anthropology. Thousands of articles from the farthest corners of Mesoamerica were traded here.

Right. Above left. Xochipilli, the "Prince of Flowers", was an Aztec god who was not only patron of the arts but also symbolized love and pleasure. National Museum of Anthropology.

Right. Above right. The figurines found on the archaeological site of Cuicuilco belong to the "pretty ladies" culture. National Museum of Anthropology.

ing water to the city and he also had a drystone wall built almost 16 km. long on the eastern edge of the city that divided the lake into two and prevented flooding in the rainy season.

The Great Temple was rebuilt yet again in 1470, and some commemorative pieces were sculpted, for instance the *Aztec Calendar*, measuring 4 meters in diameter, and the *Tizoc Stone* that celebrates battles. Both monoliths are now in the National Museum of Anthropology.

The level of the lake began to fall in the 15th century, and this led to the plan for restoring it by bringing water from the springs of Coyoacán and Churubusco via an aqueduct to distribute it through conduits to the different districts in the south of the city. Unfortunately, the extra flow increased water volume so much that it quickly became impossible to control, and the city was completely flooded.

Right. Below left. Toltec art often dealt with military subjects. This ceramic piece covered with shell mosaic represents a warrior emerging from the jaws of a coyote. National Museum of Anthropology.

Right. Below right. Olmec artists of the Gulf Coast liked to portray themselves with "baby faces" and sometimes with deformed heads. National Museum of Anthropology.

14

The Tzompantli, "altar or stockade of human skulls" was shown on panels decorating the facades of temples. Museum of the Great Temple.

Right. The Monolith Room of the Museum of the Great Temple contains a polychrome "Eagle Knight", a monumental figure of fired clay representing an Aztec warrior.

The Museum of the Great Temple was built on the site where the architectural and sculptural remains of the religious and political core of the Aztec capital were discovered.

A polychrome figure of Chac-mool, the "Messenger of the Gods", was found in the shrine dedicated to Tláloc in the Great Temple.

The only solution to this serious problem was to stop up the springs. After this disaster the Great Temple, palaces, other buildings, neighborhood temples and most of the ditches needed rebuilding.

The some 250,000 inhabitants of this lake city lived in a stratified theocratic society: priests, warriors and nobles enjoyed special privileges which were denied to the common people or *macehualtin.* While nobles did not have to pay tribute to the *Tlatoani* they held governing posts, owned land and had their own school (the *Calmecac*), the *macehualtin* or ordinary folk - the majority - were concentrated in the different *calpullis* (sectors) of the city. They paid taxes, worked the land and constructed cause-

ways, buildings and bridges. The warrior class was constantly busy with "Flowery Wars" - periodic battles to take prisoners for sacrifice in complex rites.

Access to the city was mainly by water but there were also wide causeways made of earth with gaps spanned by wooden bridges which ran to the different points of the compass. In the north was the Tepeyac causeway, the Tacuba or Tlacopan causeway ran from the center westward, communicating with the village of the same name, and in south the Iztapalapa causeway with its different branches connected with Coyoacán, Xochimilco and Tláhuac. These avenues not only linked areas but also served as dikes to control the water of the lake.

One of the most impressive examples of Aztec art is the carving of Coyolxauhqui. "She of the snake rattles on her cheeks", a moon goddess who according to legend was beheaded and dismembered. Museum of the Great Temple.

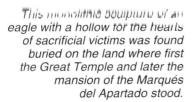

This monolithic sculpture of an eagle with a hollow for the hearts of sacrificial victims was found buried on the land where first the Great Temple and later the mansion of the Marqués del Apartado stood.

The Pyramid of the Sun measuring 65 meters in height and 225 meters along each side of its square base towers above Teotihuacan, "The Place where Men become Gods".

Right. One of the principal features of this religious complex is the spatial organization of volumes built in relation to a straight road called the "Avenue of the Dead" which ends with the Pyramid of the Moon.

The main feature of the Temple of Quetzalcóatl at Teotihuacan is the presence of numerous serpent heads, the symbol of Quetzalcóatl, the "Feathered Serpent".

One of the most striking places was the market of Tlatelolco, where the trading activity of the capital and other towns was concentrated. This large area was divided into streets and brought together some sixty thousand traders and craftsmen. There were silversmiths from Azcapotzalco, potters and jewelers from Cholula, painters from Texcoco and flower-sellers from Xochimilco, among many others. Trade in this market was by barter, but cacao beans were also used as currency. The pochtecas or merchants followed their own laws here, and many of them lived in the satellite city of Tlatelolco, which was brought under the rule of Tenochtitlan in 1473.

In 1519, when the Spanish reached the Gulf of Mexico coast and set out on their march toward the great city its main area covered 13 sq. km and contained almost 600,000 inhabitants. Moctezuma II ruled the metropolis at this time but died the same year, to be followed by Cuitláhuac who died of smallpox one month after assuming power. The last Aztec ruler was Cuauhtémoc, who directed the defense of Tenochtitlan.

One of the places that the conquistadors admired most were the gardens of the *Casas Nuevas de Moctezuma* with their House of Birds and Beasts - an exotic menagerie housing curassows, quetzals, toucans, leopards and other wild animals. But admiration was replaced by war and Cortés and his men started the downfall of the great city. In a short time the "place of colored arrows and painted shields, Tenochtitlan" died, to be reborn as a different city.

The Pyramid of Santa Cecilia Acatlán, testimony to the Toltec influence that existed in this region, stands in Tlalnepantla, State of Mexico.

Above right. View of the pyramid of Tlahuizcalpantecuhtli at Tula in the state of Hidalgo. On top stand four columns carved with warriors that originally supported the temple's roof.

Right. Below left. The circular pyramid of Cuicuilco stands in the south of Mexico City near the final spurs of the Ajusco hills.

Right. Below right. The colossal "Atlantes" testify to the Toltec people's fascination for war. These statues represent dead warriors whose duty was to accompany the sun.

Tenayuca was founded in 1224. The coatepantli or "Wall of Serpents" of its main pyramid is made up of 133 stone sculptures that form part of the structure itself rather than being just decoration.

This portrait of the conquistador Hernán Cortés wearing half armor and leaning on his sword is in the Hospital de Jesús.

An 18th-century Italian engraving of the first meeting of Cortés and the emperor Moctezuma which took place on November 8, 1519 on the Iztapalapa causeway.

THE CONQUEST OF GREAT TENOCHTITLAN

The Spanish conquest of Tenochtitlan was a not only a clash of people but also of cultures and ideas. It was a harsh meeting that served as the departure point for cementing a new ideology and nationality.

When the conquistadors under Hernán Cortés arrived in the great pre-Hispanic city they were fascinated by its impressive size and complex organization. Their amazement was so great that they would not rid themselves of the idea that this city was something out of a fairy story.

The Aztecs were a people guided by their religion and beliefs, and shortly before Cortés arrived they saw signs that foretold a great calamity. In addition, history says that they were awaiting the return of Quetzalcóatl - the god-man - a legendary white-skinned, bearded person of Toltec stock. Some of the happenings that they took as bad omens were for example a column of fire that appeared at midnight all through the year, the destruction of two temples, a comet seen in the daytime and sudden enormous waves in the lake of Texcoco. Sources also tell that a bird was killed which had a mirror on its head reflecting the skies. These ominous signs terrified the Aztec chiefs and produced a very special frame of mind.

On their way to the capital in 1519 the Spanish came across several cities that had to pay tribute to the Aztecs, and these saw the European invaders as the spearhead for an outright rebellion. And so when Cortés began his march on Mexico City he went with an army of 400 foot-soldiers, 16 horsemen and various pieces of artillery plus

Painting on wood with shell incrustations done in 1698 and now the property of the Museo de América in Madrid showing Cortes's arrival in Mexico City with his entourage.

This painting that belongs to the same series shows Moctezuma, richly attired, being carried in a litter to welcome the conquistador.

Tlaxcaltecs, Huexotzincos, Cholultecs, Tepanecs and Xochimilcos who were all eager to fight against the tribe that dominated them.

Finally Cortés and Moctezuma met. The Aztec emperor, believing at first that the Spaniard was Quetzalcóatl reborn, offered him the sacred precinct as lodging, but after a few days the conquistador took him prisoner. Meanwhile, the inhabitants of the city stayed at home, the market was closed down and an apparent calm reigned. Cortés took this opportunity to go to the Gulf coast where one of his captains, Pánfilo de Narváez, had rebelled against him.

A storm arose in the city while Cortés was away because Pedro de Alvarado, one of his soldiers, ordered an attack on the participants in a ritual ceremony in honor of *Huitzilopochtli*. Enfuriated, the population rebelled and the Spanish suddenly found themselves under siege in the Palace pf Axayácatl, but in their weakness the Aztecs allowed Cortés and his men to join them.

After a week under siege the Spanish decided to flee from Tenochtitlan in the early morning, but a women saw them and raised the alarm. The Mexica took to their canoes, attacked the flanks of the column on the march and

This scene of a bloody battle between Spaniards and Aztecs also shows how the conquistador had pre-Hispanic idols burned.

The Lienzo de Tlaxcala dating from the mid 16th century details events of the Spanish conquest and underlines the help Cortés was given by Tlaxcaltecs.

Right. Many cities in New Spain were built along Renaissance lines, employing thousands of native laborers.

destroyed the bridges over which the Spanish, loaded down with gold, hoped to make their escape. Many of them lost their lives in this flight. Tradition has it that in the town of Tacuba, when calm reigned again, Cortés sat down under a Mexican cypress and wept, since three fourths of his army had been lost in what came to be known as "The Sad Night".

After fighting off the Aztec army following them in Otumba, the Spanish decided to return to Tlaxcala, where they were well received. Meanwhile in the capital, Moctezuma died; according to some accounts he was killed by his own people, according to others, by the Spanish. The city's defense fell into the hands of Cuauhtémoc.

This last emperor was crowned during the *nemontemi* ("empty days") which according to Aztec beliefs were unlucky, so this event was considered to be a fateful omen. A few days earlier, during the brief reign of Cuitláhuac a terrible epidemic of smallpox had broken out in Mexico-Tenochtitlan, started by one of Pánfilo de Narváez's men.

With their forces regrouped, the Spanish decided to besiege the Aztec city in June 1521. By this time Cortés had a fleet of 13 brigs armed with cannons that had been built in Tlaxcala, dismantled, carried over the mountains and assembled near the capital. With these he was able to clear the lake of any enemy craft quickly and protect the army's flanks as it marched along the city's three causeways. After a short while, the conquistador changed his tactics and ordered his native allies to tear down as many buildings as they could; he cut off the supply of drinking water and filled in the ditches to give his troops clear access. The storming and burning of the Great Temple took several days of savage fighting, during which some five thousand defenders lost their lives. The Spanish forces gradually gained ground until one of the ships, commanded by captain García Holguín, captured Cuauhtémoc, who was fleeing from the fallen city by canoe. He was taken before Cortés, who was directing the last stage of the battle. Finally, on August 13, 1521, after a siege that lasted for 90 days, the great city of Mexico-Tenochtitlan fell to the conquistadors. When the Spanish arrived the Aztec culture was at its height. The tragic and heroic resistance that Tenochtitlan put up was not so much a military defense by the citizens, but a fight for their lives. Hunger, thirst, disease and wounds had weakened a people that finally disappeared.

MEXICO CITY: CAPITAL OF THE VICEROYALTY OF NEW SPAIN

After the Conquest the Spanish had the task of building a new city to honour this new province, and it was decided that it would stand on the ruins of what had been Mexico Tenochtitlan. Some of Cortés's advisers suggested that it would be better to create the city at Coyoacán, which by then had become the seat of the *Ayuntamiento* or Municipal Council, since they were well aware of the problems of being sited in a lake. However the conquistador, sensing the political, religious and administrative symbolism of the spot where the Great Temple had once stood, turned a deaf ear to their opinions. The traces of the terrible battle had hardly been cleared away when he ordered Alonso García Bravo to draw up a city plan, which in the beginning covered 100 hectares. American cities, in contrast to those of the Old World, were planned by Europeans on orderly lines, with geometrically laid out rectangular blocks and followed the Utopian models of the Renaissance. García Bravo's plan, though Renaissance in spirit, was at the same time American,

The Hospital de Jesús, founded in 1521 by Cortés himself, was the first refuge of its kind in Mexico and the entire continent.

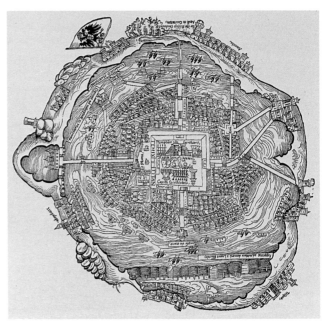

Map of Mexico City attributed to Cortés, first published in a Latin edition of his Letters to Emperor Charles V printed in Nüremberg, Germany, in 1524.

since for example he repeated the grid layout of the Aztec capital. The main lots were granted to the conquistadors - in order of rank - and to new settlers. Cortés was awarded the choicest, including the site where the *Nacional Monte de Piedad* (National Pawnshop) stands today. The native population was concentrated around the nucleus on the *chinampas* and in the former region of Tlatelolco.

The four pre-Hispanic quarters were kept, but now with Christianized names: Santa María Cuepopan, San Sebastián Atzacoalco, San Pablo Zoquipan and San Juan Moyotlán. The city was crisscrossed by channels that were traveled by canoes carrying drinking water, food and people. In 1552, the Tacuba causeway was still one of the city's main thoroughfares, but it was now paved and the houses that lined it were occupied by all types of craftsmen, such as painters, shoemakers, tailors, carpen-

ters, candlemakers and bakers. The different religious orders - Franciscans, Augustinians and Dominicans, etc, - established themselves on the best land in the city.

In the first years of the infant capital, government was in the hands of a Municipal Council and two Courts of Appeal *(Audiencias)*. However problems between these different authorities led to the emperor Charles V ordering that the territory was to be ruled by a viceroy representing the Spanish monarchy. The first viceroy of New Spain was Antonio de Mendoza, who was succeeded by 61 more governors until 1821, the year in which Mexico became independent from Spain. In 1548 the metropolis was given the title of "Most Noble, Distinguished, Most Loyal and Imperial City of Mexico"

Pre-Hispanic buildings were demolished, the causeways restored, the streets cleared of rubble and the Chapultepec

MEXICO.

A series of similar works appeared after the Nüremberg map. The lower part of this illustration shows three high ranking men. The costume of the center figure identifies him as a native prince.

This screen dating from the early years of the viceregal period shows various buildings in Mexico City and scenes from the everyday life of its inhabitants.

Above right. The beauty and coquettishness of the women of New Spain is set off against the fruit and vegetables sold by natives in this 1864 lithograph.

Below right. One of the most picturesque places in colonial Mexico was the Paseo de la Viga where citizens gathered to stroll along the canal banks or enjoy boat rides.

This lithograph dating from 1840 shows Mexico City cathedral and four persons dressed in the clothes typical of the period.

Above right. Mexico City cathedral took over three centuries to build and so the dominant styles of most periods are represented in this impressive religious monument.

aqueduct repaired - the shortage of drinking water was still a problem - and the ditches were cleaned out. In short, the ancient city's amenities were restored and other essential ones added.

The first houses of the Spanish were like small castles, with fortified towers, battlements and drawbridges over the channels because the threat of an Indian rebellion still loomed. Cortés had the Shipyards built, fortified places that protected the city and guarded the brigs at the same time. In the course of time these buildings changed and came to have resplendent facades. The metropolis sprouted towers that dominated houses; with the constant coming and going of watercraft and people the city was an anthill of activity.

The original city plan was soon too small and it was expanded successively. When waves of European immigrants in search of fortune arrived, mills, inns and work-

shops appeared where craftsmen's guilds were organized which became the basis for the productive activity of the colonial city.

By the late 16th century 35 buildings had been completed or were underway, including the Royal Palace, home of the viceroy and the *Audiencia*, today the National Palace; the headquarters of the Municipal Council; the old cathedral and the beginnings of the new one, the Archbishop's Palace, the University, and the Purísima Concepción Hospital or Hospital de Jesús, founded by Cortés himself. Other hospitals were established as the years went by: for example San Juan de Dios for the indigent, San José de los Naturales for Indians, San Lázaro for lepers and the Hospital del Amor de Dios which treated venereal diseases.

Buildings that date from the 17th and 18th centuries characteristically use *tezontle* and limestone. *Tezontle* - a dark

*The cathedral is
spectacularly
illuminated for
important civic and
religious celebrations.*

35

The Metropolitan Sagrarium built in the 17th century has one of the most remarkable carved limestone facades in all New Spain.

Above right. The National Palace, today the seat of the highest powers of the Mexican government, was originally built as a residence for viceroys.

Below right. The main courtyard of the National Palace. The Act of Independence was signed in one of its many rooms.

red volcanic stone that is light in weight and easy to work - was used either cut into slabs for masonry work or split into sheets for facings. It was taken from the nearby hills of Santa Marta and El Peñón. Doorways, window frames and balconies were made of a gray limestone known as *chiluca*.

Colonial population was a colorful picturesque mix: peninsular Spaniards, their children born in America, called *criollos*, *mestizos* (Spanish-Mexican), foreigners, Indians, negroes, mulattos and Chinese together with the "castes", racial mixes of certain of these groups. The city is calculated to have contained some fifty thousand inhabitants by the mid 17th century.

Since the city was surrounded by lakes it was in constant danger from flooding. Eight terrible catastrophes of this kind happened in its history, three before the Conquest and five during the Viceroyalty. The worse one occurred

in 1629, when the city streets and squares were filled with boats for about five years because it was impossible to move around on foot.

Some of the most important buildings of this century were the many convents, with their various cloisters, locutories and some with separate cells - like small houses - for nuns from wealthy backgrounds. There were 16 convents, eight of which had been founded in the 16th century. The oldest was the Convento de la Concepción, and its branches were Regina, Jesús María, Balvanera, San José de Gracia, San Bernardo and La Encarnación. In the course of time the convents of San Jerónimo, Santa Inés, Santa Clara, Santa Catalina, San Lorenzo, Santa Brígida, Corpus Christi and others were built. The most important were the convents of Jesús María and San Jerónimo. The first was a royal convent since an illegitimate daughter of king Philip II lived there. Sor Juana Inés de la Cruz, the

View of Constitution Square, popularly known as the "Zócalo", the everlasting religious, political and administrative nerve center of Mexico City.

most outstanding literary figure of the viceregal period, took her vows in the convent of San Jerónimo in 1669.

The most important churches in the colonial city were Santo Domingo, San Agustín, San Francisco, Santa Catalina, Santa Veracruz, San José, San Miguel, San Fernando, San Hipólito and Santa María la Redonda. However, the most important building raised in the period was definitely the cathedral, which was solemnly dedicated for a second time in 1667. Its beginnings were modest - a small church built with the remains of the great Aztec *Teocalli*. In 1530 it was elevated to the rank of diocese and to archdiocese in 1545. History tells that it took forty years to lay the foundations of the new church. The architect of the ground plan was Claudio de Arciniega, who designed five naves, the central one higher and wider than the lateral ones. The main facade was finished in the second half of the 17th century. Inside, the *Altar de los Reyes* (Altar of the Kings), a masterpiece of New Spanish baroque created by Jerónimo de Balbás in

1718, is breathtakingly beautiful. In the same century the architect Lorenzo Rodríguez built the Capilla del Sagrario onto the Cathedral, which was consecrated in 1768 and has a marvellous facade of limestone.

The towers were completed in the late 18th century when they were topped with two enormous stone bell-shaped structures. At present, although the church is being restored, visitors can still admire the imposing architecture, its 14 richly decorated chapels and its priceless treasures.

What is now the National Palace is, together with the cathedral, one of the most important buildings in the city. Originally constructed as the residence of viceroys, it stands on the site of the Casas Nuevas of Moctezuma and has been altered several times since the mid 16th century. In 1692 a mutiny broke out that caused tremendous damage to the building and it had to be shored up. In the 18th century the noted architect Pedro de Arrieta directed important alterations, and finally in 1926 another story was added.

An 1840 lithograph showing a couple with their little daughter strolling on Santo Domingo square in front of the convent of the Dominicans, one of the orders that converted New Spain to Christianity.

Left. The second most important colonial square after the Zócalo is Santo Domingo, surrounded by Santo Domingo church, the Palace of the Inquisition, the old Customs House and the "Evangelists Arcade".

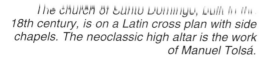

The church of Santo Domingo, built in the 18th century, is on a Latin cross plan with side chapels. The neoclassic high altar is the work of Manuel Tolsá.

View of the interior of La Enseñanza church whose altarpieces are among the finest examples of 18th-century baroque.

Above left. The courtyard of the building that was the Palace of the Inquisition in the colonial period and later the School of Medicine of the University of Mexico.

Left. Below left. The coat of arms of the Inquisition can still be seen on the facade of its Palace.

Left. Below right. The house of the counts of Heras Soto has one of the most beautiful corners in Mexico City, a work of lace carved in stone.

La Enseñanza church was dedicated in 1778 as part of an institution for the education of women in colonial times.

The greatest humanists of the viceregal period studied in the College of San Ildefonso, which now houses one of Mexico City's newest museums.

Above right. The old Customs building on Santo Domingo square was begun in 1729 but originally founded to manage taxes in the 16th century.

Below right. Left and right. La Profesa church is a gem of 18th-century architecture where young Jesuits took their vows. The neoclassic high altar is the work of Manuel Tolsá.

The Royal and Pontifical University of New Spain, modeled directly on the University of Salamanca, was opened by the viceroy Luis de Velasco in 1553. It had four faculties: Arts, Theology, Medicine, and Canons and Law. From 1597 on, graduates enjoyed the same privileges as those given by Spanish universities, and during the three centuries that the Colony lasted the Royal and Pontifical University was a shining example of discipline and academic excellence. There were other schools in addition to this institution, for example San Ildefonso, San Pedro y San Pablo, the Colegio de Niñas and the college of San Ramón Nonato.

To return to the 17th century, a great aqueduct was built between 1603 and 1620 that carried water from the village of Santa Fe and emptied into a basin located very near where the Palace of Fine Arts *(Palacio de las Bellas Artes)* stands today. There were also numerous public and private fountains fed by both the Santa Fe and Chapultepec aqueducts, and at the same period a large number of water carriers would regularly deliver from house to house for a modest sum of money.

Celebrations of a religious nature were common in the social round of New Spain. There were processions and there were dramatic recitations and religious plays in church atriums; dramas were performed in squares, theaters or the Sala de Comedias. There were also masquerades, where people dressed as mythological figures, there were gatherings at shrines and there were bullfights. On foot or in elegant carriages, citizens went to the different "promenades" or parks *(paseos)*. The oldest was the Alameda, created by order of the viceroy Luis de Velasco II in 1590, a tree-shaded area which still exists in the city

The lovely courtyard of the Colegio de las Vizcaínas, built in the 18th century to shelter widows and orphan girls of Basque origin has simple slender arcades of a delicate elegance.

Right. The 18th-century Capilla del Pocito behind the old Basilica of Guadalupe. This building by the architect Francisco Guerrero y Torres has an unusual elliptical ground plan.

Entry to the church of the ex-convent of San Francisco is through the baroque doorway of Balvanera chapel.

The house of the counts of the Valley of Orizaba, popularly known as the "House of Tiles" is a fine example of an 18th-century residence.

This lithograph dating from 1864 shows the "House of Tiles" in the background and in the foreground the square and the mansion of the Marquis of Santa Fe de Guardiola which stood until this century.

center. The Paseo de la Viga, the Paseo Nuevo or Bucareli and Chapultepec Park were equally places where the inhabitants of Mexico City whiled away peaceful hours.

The Basilica of Guadalupe was built in the mid 17th century to house the image of Our Lady of Guadalupe, who according to legend appeared in 1531, after it had been kept in other places. The exquisite Capilla del Pocito dates from the 18th century and is built around waters that were believed to have miraculous powers. In the same century the city was enhanced by several new churches whose impressive baroque altarpieces can still be admired today: La Enseñanza, Regina, La Profesa, San Francisco, San Felipe Neri and Santísima Trinidad are just a few examples of where this style flowered in both facades and interiors. Mansions dating from viceregal times such as the house of the counts of San Mateo de Valparaíso on Isabel la Católica street, the mansion of the count of the Valley of Orizaba - better known as the House of Tiles - the residence of the counts of Santiago

de Calimaya, now the Mexico City Museum, and the home of the counts of Herrero Soto testify to the transformations that the city underwent in this century.

Life in the great houses of New Spain was centered around lovely patios: the ground floor was the province of servants - always numerous - while the family lived on the floor above. In addition to ordinary rooms, houses had a Reception Salon where distinguished visitors were welcomed. Houses also boasted grand staircases, coffered ceilings, heavy window drapes, furniture of precious woods, brocades imported from Europe and Asia, gold and silver, screens and other luxury items. These fine residences also had outbuildings on the ground floor that served as stores, storerooms, stables, service rooms or offices.

Some civic buildings constructed or altered in the 18th century were the Palace of the Municipal Council, the Tribunal of the Inquisition, built by Pedro de Arrieta on a corner of Santo Domingo square, and the College of San Ignacio or Vizcaínas, which provided a home for orphan girls and widows of Basque origin.

The distinguished house of the Marquis de Jaral de Berrio, built in 1779 was inhabited by Agustín de Iturbide during the First Empire.

Above right. The only castle in Mexico City is Chapultepec, the residence of Emperor Maximilian during his brief reign.

Right. Below left and right. Two views of the Salto del Agua Fountain in 1864 and today. The water was channeled to it from Chapultepec via an aqueduct.

The high society of different times strolled along Plateros street (now Francisco I. Madero) in front of the Palace of Iturbide.

*In the south of the city are the 17th-century church
and ex-convent of the Carmelites.*

The colonial city rose to its greatest splendor under two remarkable viceroys. The first was Antonio María de Bucareli, who governed from 1771 to 1779, and the second Juan Vicente de Güemes y Pacheco, the second count of Revillagigedo, who ruled over the territory of New Spain from 1789 to 1794.

Some of the improvements carried out by Bucareli were the continuation of drainage works begun in the 17th century, the remodeling of the Mint - built in 1734 and expanded by Miguel Contansó in the late 19th century - and various alterations to the Customs House and the Prison of La Acordada that stood opposite the Alameda Central. He also had a wide, tree-lined avenue built that connected the haciendas in the south with the city center. The National Pawn Shop, an important charity institution created thanks to the initiative and financial sponsorship of Pedro Romero de Terreros, was also opened during this viceroy's times.

Some time later, when the second count of Revillagigedo was governing, priority was given to restoring the capital, and from then on it had a new system of street lighting,

drainage, paved streets, sidewalks and garbage deposits. Revillagigedo created the great Volador Market and organized the first population census of New Spain, which gave the number of inhabitants as 4,483,569. It was during his term of government that two of the most important relics of the Aztec culture were discovered: the statue of *Coatlicue* and the *Aztec Calendar* which both came to light in 1790 when the Main Square was being remodeled. In 1793 the engineer Diego García Conde drew a plan of the city, one of the most accurate of the times, which shows that the capital was bounded in the south by what is now Fray Servando Teresa de Mier Avenue, in the east by the Anillo de Circunvalación, in the north by the Glorieta of Peralvillo, and in the west by the Alameda Central. García Conde reported that the city had 397 streets and lanes, 78 squares large and small, 14 parish churches, 41 convents, 80 major schools and 8 hospitals.

A few years earlier, in 1783, the San Carlos Academy of Noble Arts had been founded by order of Charles III. With the creation of this institution the canons and teach-

The upper story of La Merced cloister, built in the 18th century, is considered to be one of the most beautiful in Mexico due to its rich decoration.

The Franciscan convent and church of San Diego were built in the 16th century in Churubusco. Now housing the National Museum of Interventions, it was the scene of a battle against North American troops in 1847.

*On June 27, 1797 Manuel Tolsá was appointed
construction engineer of the Royal Mining Seminary,
a neoclassic work finished in 1813.*

ing of the arts underwent a radical transformation. The old system of apprenticeship in studios was replaced by collective instruction in official schools. In the classrooms of this academy, students were confronted by impressive plaster statues from Europe, such as the *Laocoon* which served them as models.

The 19th century began tumultuously in Mexico: in 1810 the War of Independence broke out that was to strip the Spanish crown of all its power in these American lands. As a result of the warfare there was a mass migration of peasants into the city, which produced certain signs of overcrowding, especially on the outskirts. In time, villages such as San Angel, Coyoacán, Mixcoac and Tlalpan - formerly known as San Agustín de las Cuevas - found themselves becoming more and more part of the city.

War years are always a rather barren period as far as urban or architectural development is concerned, since people are preoccupied with the problems of the moment. Nevertheless, it was in this period that a new style was launched which toppled the baroque from the dominant position it had held for the two previous centuries: neoclassic. The recently created Academy was the seedbed for works in this style. In the cathedral Manuel Tolsá created the dome of the transept, the clocktower, some sculptures, balustrades and finishes in the neoclassic style without spoiling the harmony of the structure. Tolsá also erected several buildings, such as the Palace of Minería - finished in 1813 - the house of the Marquis del Apartado, the mansion of the Counts of Buenavista (today the San Carlos Museum) and the equestrian statue of Charles IV, popularly known as *El Caballito* (The Little Horse). Clean-lined columns, friezes with triglyphs and metopes plus triangular pediments began to appear not only in the capital but all over the new nation.

The National Art Museum, formerly
the Palace of Communications,
houses an extensive collection of
19th and 20th-century paintings and
sculptures. The building by the Italian
Silvio Contri is in a Renaissance style
reminiscent of Florentine palaces.

The equestrian monument to King
Charles IV of Spain the work of
Tolsá, was cast in 1803. The statue
was originally intended to stand in
the center of the Plaza Mayor. Ever
since it was unveiled it has been
popularly known as "El Caballito"
(The Little Horse).

The Museum of Applied Arts, which houses the belongings of the antiques collector Franz Mayer, stands next to the 18th-century church of San Juan de Dios.

Right. Above right. The first stone of the church of the Santísima Trinidad was laid in 1755. Its baroque facade with slender pilasters extols various religious themes and dogmas.

Right. Below left. The church of San Hipólito was built in the mid 18th century. A stone in one corner of its small atrium commemorates the tragic "Sad Night".

Right. Above left. The house of the counts of Santiago de Calimaya, a fine example of 18th-century civic architecture, is now Mexico City Museum.

Right. Below right. The Palace of Axayácatl and later the residence of Cortés formerly stood on the site of the National Pawnshop.

58

The 18th century alcove of the Virgin of Loreto at Tepotzotlán is one of the most resplendent gems of baroque art on the entire continent.

Left. The Society of Jesus, the most powerful order in New Spain founded the College of San Francisco Xavier of Tepotzotlán in the 17th and 18th centuries, which is now the National Museum of the Viceroyalty.

The altarpieces of Tepotzotlán are considered to be New Spain's most magnificent.

R.d la M. Sor María Engracia Josefa del S.mo Rosario, Monja profesa de velo y coro en el Conv.to
de Sta. Teresa de esta Ciudad de Guadal.a Hija leg.ma de D.

The ex-convent of Acolman, a fine example of 16th-century monastic architecture, is not far from Mexico City.

Left. Above left. Colonial sculpture is well represented by this alabaster statue of St. Sebastian. National Museum of the Viceroyalty.

Left. Above right. An 18th-century gold filigree monstrance in the Museum of Tepotzotlán.

Left. Below left. Images of Christ made of corn stalk pith combine pre-Hispanic techniques with others of European origin. National Museum of the Viceroyalty.

Left. Below right. One of the most striking genres of New Spain's painting is that of "Flowered" or "Crowned Nuns". National Museum of the Viceroyalty.

Atrium crosses like this one in Cuautitlán played an important role in the teachings of the first religious orders to arrive in New Spain.

Iturbide Market shown in this 19th-century lithograph was one of the many commercial centers that have existed in Mexico City throughout its history.

Right. This aerial view of a present-day market shows that Mexicans have not changed their buying habits much.

Well-to-do people, here represented by two attractive women wearing mantillas, would visit the capital's markets where vendors offered their services.

THE MODERN PRESENT-DAY CAPITAL

In the years following the War of Independence, Mexico City went through a period of instability that caused a drop in the number of new buildings. Even the San Carlos Academy went into decline because of the shortage of funds. However, its situation changed in 1843 when President Antonio López de Santa Anna ordered its reorganization. He was also the one who planned a monument to the Independence for the center of the Main Square, to be built by Lorenzo de la Hidalga. However, Santa Anna's regime fell, and only the base or socle (*zócalo*) of the column was ever constructed. From this time onward the square, a gathering place, came to be called the "Zócalo", which is still its popular name today. There were several forms of government between 1821 and 1930: a very brief empire under Agustín de Iturbide and another short-lived one under Maximilian of

Hapsburg; a Republic, established by Benito Juárez, and the 30-year dictatorship of General Porfirio Díaz. These were years of bitter struggles between Conservatives and Liberals and of foreign interventions.

In 1824 the Federal Constitutional Council decided that the residence of heads of state should be Mexico City, and thus the Federal District was born. In November of the same year it was decided that this would occupy an area two leagues in radius from the central square. The limits were extended in 1845 by a decree stipulating the inclusion of villages, small-holdings, farms and properties lying within the new boundaries - regulations that changed over time. The city then covered some 15.3 sq. km.

The Reform Laws passed in 1856 were instrumental in changing both the physiognomy and function of the capital. The 1861 Law Confiscating and Nationalizing Church Property changed the landholding pattern to a great extent. The large Church properties were sold off to the public, and this led to a fresh spate of building.

The enormous convents were split and streets were dri-

Tall buildings harmonize with a modernistic "Little Horse" on this city avenue.

Left. Mexico City's great avenues date from earlier times but have been modified or widened to ease the flow of traffic.

An example of modern architecture — Mexico's World Trade Center — with the Siqueiros Cultural Polyforum in the foreground.

The renowned 19th-century landscape painter José María Velasco (1840 - 1912) captured the splendor of the Valley of Mexico and the city of the time in this sweeping view.

Following page. Although the valley has changed considerably since Velasco's times, Mexico City is still impressive and forward-looking.

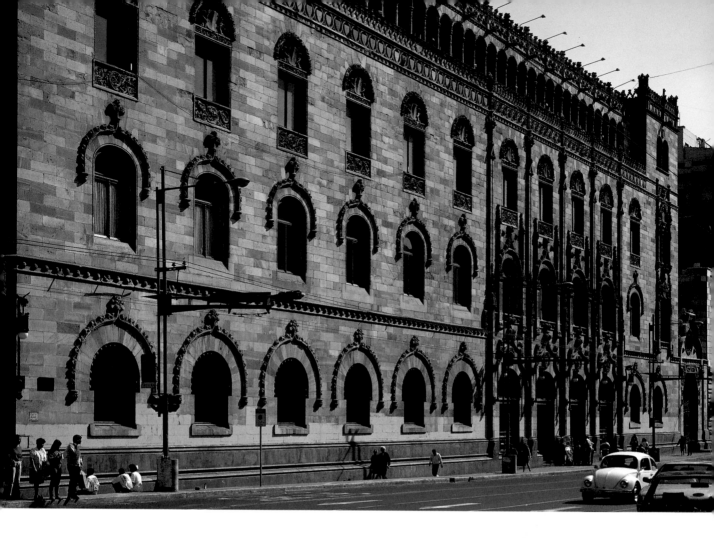

ven through them; some religious buildings became public - for example the church of San Agustín became the National Library, the Colegio de la Santa Cruz de Tlatelolco ended as a prison. The convent of Capuchinas was torn down for the sake of Lerdo street (today Palmas). Leandro Valle street was driven through the convent of Santo Domingo, and San Bernardo was divided to make place for Ocampo.

On June 12, 1864 Maximilian of Hapsburg, the Austrian Emperor of Mexico and his wife Charlotte (Carlota) made their ceremonial entry into Mexico City, witnessed by thousands of people of all classes. Yet only a few short years later, on June 19, 1867, Maximilian would be executed by a firing squad on the outskirts of Querétaro. During his brief reign Maximilian made some changes to the capital. He altered Chapultepec Castle to make it his residence and in 1865 had the "Paseo de la Emperatriz" created, an avenue that cut through the city's rectangular grid pattern. This "imperial" promenade is one of the busiest and most beautiful thoroughfares of the city today: the Paseo de la Reforma.

When Porfirio Díaz came to power not only the capital but the whole country experienced an unprecedented period of modernization. The official culture encouraged by this government aimed to please the aristocracy at the same time as it defined its new ideology. The political stability brought about by the thirty-year regime was reflected in a boom in building. Foreign architects and artists flocked to the capital during this period, bringing with them new construction techniques and materials, including reinforced concrete. The entire country blossomed with public works such as roads, bridges, markets, railroads and ports.

As for the environment, the excessive tree felling that had been going on for over four hundred years was challenged at the beginning of the 20th century when a group of people headed by the engineer Miguel Angel de Quevedo formed the *Sociedad Forestal* (Forest Society) which promoted the protection of woodlands and forests. It was at this time that Chapultepec Park became a leisure area.

The arrival of Europeans, together with President Díaz's predilection for everything French, gradually transformed

The Siqueiros Cultural Polyforum, with mural painting and an original decoration by this revolutionary artist, is a building that defies orthodox architectural canons.

Left. The Main Post Office, which stands on the site of the Hospital Real de Terceros was begun in 1902 under the direction of the architect Adamo Boari.

One of the city's most eye-catching buildings is the Stock Exchange whose arrow-shaped profile towers over Reforma Avenue.

"El Papalote" children's museum is popular with visitors from both the capital and the rest of the country.

Right. Mexico City's large arteries, enormous traffic circles and wide avenues are always full of vehicles.

The Hemicycle built in honor of Benito Juárez is a beautiful monument on one side of the Alameda Park. Its architect, Guillermo Heredia, chose white Carrara marble for it.

Above left. The Aztec Stadium is one of the largest sports facilities, seating up to 110,000 spectators.

The Sports Palace, a geodesic dome covered with copper sheets, was built for the 1968 Olympic Games.

Below left. The Olympic Stadium in the University City with its decoration by Diego Rivera is one of the most notable examples of the search to combine art with architecture.

the city. Several buildings appeared that had a skeleton of rolled iron, and the most spectacular use made of this material is to be seen in the University Museum of El Chopo. Some Art Nouveau elements were incorporated into buildings such as the Centro Mercantil, now the Hotel de la Ciudad de México, as well as many houses in the Juárez and Roma districts. Veneers and finishes of materials such as Italian marble, bronze or granite became fashionable.

Together with French taste, another style appeared that researchers have named "Neo-indigenous" since it combines different elements originating from Aztec, Maya and Mixtec architecture. One of the clearest examples of this fondness for pre-Hispanic shapes is the Cuauhtémoc Monument, unveiled in 1887, which takes its inspiration from Aztec art.

In the field of urban development, from the mid 19th to the early 20th centuries, many entrepreneurs discovered that real estate was a highly profitable business. Between 1824 and 1930 these investors created the first housing developments or residential districts in the city. The first one we have documentary information about is Los Azulejos, established in part of what is now the Santa María la Ribera quarter, while the Guerrero area arose on the grounds that had belonged to the convent of San Fernando. Other districts were created between 1900 and 1910 such as Cuauhtémoc, Roma, Condesa, Juárez and El Chopo. Some of these did not follow the grid pattern, since each one was designed in isolation adopting all types of layouts, which led to a certain geometrical disorder as a whole. Many large residences in those new areas combined features of country houses with the demands of modernity. At the turn of the century the capital had half a million inhabitants.

To celebrate the Hundredth Anniversary of Mexico's Independence in 1910 Porfirio Díaz, who was then 80

The University City marks the culmination of modern architecture in Mexico. The Main Library shown here is decorated with a mural by Juan O'Gorman.

The central plaza of the National University is dominated by the Rectoría, a fourteen-story tower standing on the highest part of the campus.

On one side of the Rectoría David Alfaro Siqueiros did two "sculpture-paintings": reliefs covered with glass mosaic.

The perfect blending of architecture and sculpture is a salient feature of the Revolution Monument.

years old, had a large number of monuments erected. The most important of these was the Independence Column, dedicated on September 16 of the same year. Other commemorative buildings belonging to this significant date are the Manicomio Central, erected on the former hacienda of La Castañeda and the Escuela Normal Primaria para Maestros, both works by the head of state's son. The Juárez Hemicycle was inaugurated and the first stone was laid of the Legislative Palace, which was in fact never finished. In 1938 the dome intended for this building was placed on the top of the Revolution Monument, a work by the architect Carlos Obregón Santacilia. In the same period work was carried out in drainage, paving, new streets, lighting and water supply.

Penitentiaries were built along modern American lines in an effort to fight against crime. The most important of these was Lecumberri Prison, designed by the architect Antonio Torres Torija and opened in 1900. Remodeling

of the building began in 1977 and since 1982 it has housed the National Archives where Mexico's vast collection of historical documents is kept.

The National University was also opened in 1910, and in the course of time became the supreme center of studies in Mexico. The headquarters were in the city center, scattered among different buildings in what was known as the Student Quarter. The same year the Mexican Revolution broke out, marking the end of Porfirio Díaz's era.

The armed struggle held back the city's growth for several years. When the fighting ended, land demand increased in most cities as a result of the concentration of sources of employment. Mexico City, which by now held almost 740,000 inhabitants, needed all the urban amenities, and one of the actions taken as a result in the 1920's was the introduction of public transportation. Little by little, villages that until this time had had been largely independent of the city were drawn into it.

The Monument to Race looks like a pre-Columbian pyramid and is topped by a bronze eagle.

Left. Mexico City has grown impressively over the years.

This group of statues commemorating the foundation of Mexico-Tenochtitlan stands at the side of one of the buildings that house City Government offices.

This modern section of new Chapultepec Park enhances the city and the surrounding mountains.

One of the most interesting urban projects dates from 1922, when the architect José Luis Cuevas took on the housing development of *Lomas de Chapultepec* or Chapultepec Heights as it was known at the beginning. This district was created in a hilly area near the famous park and nowadays is one of the most elegant residential areas in the city. A few years later, in 1925, the Hipódromo Condesa district was established which included open tree-covered areas that had never been seen before in other districts.

As a result of the Revolution, the State instituted a nationalist policy in the 1920's aimed at recovering the legacy of viceregal times as a means to achieve national solidarity. One of the key figures in this cultural policy was the humanist José Vasconcelos who not only had neocolonial buildings erected but also enthusiastically promoted Mexico's most outstanding pictorial movement: muralism.

Vasconcelos, as Secretary of Education under President Alvaro Obregón, offered artists the walls of several buildings. Diego Rivera was given the amphitheater of the National Preparatory School, an institution located where the College of San Ildefonso had once stood. The painter interpreted the ideas of Vasconcelos in "The Creation", a pictorial hymn to rationalism and man's intellectual powers. José Clemente Orozco painted his famous mural "The Trench" in the same school, which embodies his vision of the Revolutionary epic. David Alfaro Siqueiros,

This 19th-century engraving shows people of different social levels in the Alameda Central, traditionally one of the most popular leisure areas in the city at all periods.

Left. When it was constructed in the fifties the Latin American Tower, here seen from the Alameda, was the tallest building in the city.

Statues or monuments dedicated to the great figures of pre-Hispanic times can be found all over the city. This one is of the Emperor Itzcóatl, who had the Tepeyac causeway built in 1429.

IZCOATL

Many groups of statues stand in the Alameda Park. This one is of the Danaids who according to classical mythology strive in vain to fill their pitchers with water to purify themselves.

Above right. The Dolores Olmedo Museum in the south of the city houses a large collection of works by Diego Rivera and Frida Kahlo as well as almost 600 pre-Hispanic pieces.

Below right. The Dolores Olmedo Museum located on what used to be La Noria estate in Xochimilco also contains many pieces of popular art such as the traditional "Trees of Life".

The bronze figure of Neptune, God of the Sea, graces one of the many tree-shaded areas of the Alameda.

In the thirties, Diego Rivera planned the Anahuacalli, the "House of Anáhuac". The spacious main room of this museum was the artist's studio.

The famous painter Frida Kahlo lived in the Coyoacán district. Her house, now a museum, contains some paintings by Diego Rivera and his bedroom.

The wheelchair and easel where the tormented painter Frida Kahlo worked are preserved in her Museum-House where Diego Rivera lived from the late twenties to the mid fifties.

The Frida Kahlo museum houses several of her personal belongings: the Mexican dresses she loved so much, oils by Diego Rivera, and the bed where she had to spend long periods.

The National Auditorium, a modern forum that can hold almost ten thousand has 27 entrances and a monumental half-covered foyer.

Right. A modern hotel zone stands on the Paseo de la Reforma.

The Fuente de Petróleos was built to commmemorate the expropriation of oil decreed by President Lázaro Cárdenas in 1938.

another famous Mexican muralist, was given the walls of the small courtyard to paint his mural "The Myths". Other places decorated with murals dating from this period are the walls of the National Palace, the headquarters of the Ministry of Education, the colonial building of the Colegio de San Pedro y San Pablo and the Benito Juárez School.

At this time a group of artists organized the Union of Workers, Technicians, Painters and Sculptors that rejected individualism and easel painting. They proposed socializing art through monumental works of a public nature containing a message that would give stimulus to the people's struggle against the bourgeoisie. These ideas are clearly expressed in many works of the period.

One of the trends that began to win support in the city in the mid 1920's was Art Deco, a movement originating in France that took root in the capital. In most cases, this style used decorative elements taken from pre-Hispannic design: stepped compositions, high and low relief, and geometric lines. One of the best examples of this is the Palace of Fine Arts which, although begun by the Italian architect Adamo Boari in 1904 was decorated in the 1930's by Federico Mariscal, who was inspired by pre-Hispanic features.

Road building flourished. The third decade of this century saw the 20 de Noviembre Avenue opened; the Viaducto Miguel Alemán was built in the late forties, the Calzada de Tlalpán in the fifties and a stretch of the Anillo Periferico in the sixties.

A population shift from the central area to the outskirts, mainly in the south and southwest, began in the period between 1940 and 1950, and there was intensive industrialization, particularly in the north of the city. Since 1951 the urban area has spilled over the limits of the Federal

Above left. The Christopher Columbus Monument dedicated by Porfirio Díaz in 1877 stands on the Paseo de la Reforma. It includes five bronze statues.

Above right. Mexico City contains different monuments in artistic harmony with the modern buildings around them.

The monument to the Emperor Cuauhtémoc inaugurated in 1887 stands on the road island where Reforma and Insurgentes Avenues cross.

One of the most beautiful statues in Mexico City is Diana the Huntress, a work cast in bronze some three meters tall.

The sculptor Manuel Olaguíbel who created the statue thought of it as representing an Amazon and called it The Archeress of the North, but ever since it was inaugurated it has been popularly known as Diana the Huntress.

In 1758 work began to rebuild what had been the retreat of the viceroys and what we know today as Chapultepec Castle, surrounded by the Park of the same name. Important events in Mexican history have taken place here.

The castle now contains a museum which among other things fron different periods houses objects that decorated the rooms during the brief reign of Maximilian and Carlota in the latter half of the 19th century.

Above right. Mural painting by David Alfaro Siqueiros in Chapultepec Castle showing Porfirio Díaz surrounded by the society of the time.

Below right. The Casa del Lago, an important cultural center, was built on the banks of the smaller Chapultepec lake.

District into the State of Mexico. By the fifties, the population of the capital was three million.

In 1942 the government ordered rents to be frozen, a move promoted by the president, Manuel Avila Camacho. This meant that for many years rents could not be raised; tenants protected under the order could not be evicted and their descendents could inherit the contract.

During the administration of Miguel Alemán (1946 - 1952), a time of prosperity, the city was given a new face. One of the greatest architectural and urban projects not only of the Alemán era but of the entire 20th century was the *Ciudad Universitaria* (University City), the new home of the National University. This outstanding work is a focus and watershed of modern history.

The University City symbolized the values of a post-Revolutionary regime that was striving for modernity without rejecting nationalistic ideas. The new seat of the University broke the limits of the city which by then was beginning to eat up neighboring towns. Insurgentes Avenue, the longest in the capital, linked the various districts with the burgeoning south.

Several different trends predominate in the University complex: on one hand strict functionalism based largely on Bauhaus principles and Le Corbusier's ideas, and on the other, a more flexible and less austere modernism. A third aspect was provided by the individual projects of people such as Juan O'Gorman, creator of the Central Library, Augusto Pérez Palacios, with his Olympic

Many ever-popular activities can still be enjoyed in Chapultepec Park. Young and old like to fly balloons, feed the birds, eat cotton candy and set pinwheels spinning.

Above left. The Monument to the Boy Heroes stands at one of the entrances to Chapultepec Park. It commemorates the heroic defense of the castle by cadets of the Military Academy in 1847.

Below left. The amusement park in New Chapultepec Park is one of the most exciting in the city, boasting a spectacular roller coaster, among other attractions.

Chapultepec Zoo houses animals from all over the world, living contentedly in faithful reproductions of their habitats.

President Porfirio Díaz had a special monument erected to commemorate the Centennial of the Independence. This is how the "Angel" was born, no doubt the best-loved statue in all the city.

Right. The overhead view of the Angel towering above the Paseo de la Reforma has become an emblem of Mexico City.

Reforma Avenue is enhanced by the Independence Column crowned by a statue of a Winged Victory 6.70 meters tall that weighs 7 tons.

Mexico City is a complex network where past and present are woven together by its buildings, avenues, monuments and very own characteristic features.

Above left. The building most symbolical of Mexico City after the cathedral is probably the Palace of Fine Arts built between 1904 and 1934, an excellent example of the Art Déco style.

José Clemente Orazco painted the work called Catharsis where he strongly criticizes the corruption of a superficial society without scruples.

Below left. Some important works of great Mexican muralists such as David Alfaro Siqueiros are to be seen inside the Palace of Fine Arts. This one entitled The New Democracy is in pyroxylin and was painted in the mid forties.

Rufino Tamayo also painted in the Palace of Fine Arts, using warm, strong and delicate colors, with clever and subtle monochromatic interplays full of unsuspected contrasts.

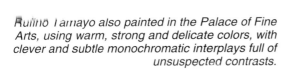

Stadium, and Alberto T. Arai's obviously pre-Hispanic inspired facades. The University City was a single undertaking that brought architects with different or opposing ideas together. It was also in more than one sense the culmination of more than twenty years of modern Mexican architecture and the concrete expression of a different view.

The most remarkable features of the University City are the way local materials are used and how the plastic arts are combined. Materials include volcanic lava from the area known as the Pedregal, used for paving, stairways, foundations and facings. The integration of plastic ele-

ments, one of the ideas taken from nationalism to give art more mass appeal, can be seen in buildings where architecture, sculpture and painting produce a pleasing unity. Artists such as David Alfaro Siqueiros, José Chávez Morado and Juan O'Gorman were some of the main followers of this trend.

Although work actually began in 1950, a symbolic foundation ceremony took place in 1952, and the first faculties were moved from the city center to their new home in 1954. This outstanding complex was built on about two million square meters (some 750 acres) of the six million (1,800 acres) expropriated. In addition to the National

In his mural Dream of a Sunday Afternoon in the Alameda Park Rivera captured the lighthearted atmosphere of the spot. In the center is the Fashionable Skeleton holding the hand of Diego Rivera as a boy.

Autonomous University and other universities both public and private the city has another important center of learning: the National Polytechnic Institute, created under a decree issued by President Lázaro Cárdenas in 1937.

Thanks to new techniques for foundations the authorities allowed taller and taller buildings to be erected. The Latin American Tower, finished in 1952, was the tallest steel-frame structure of its time. Since then, other skyscrapers have been built such as the Pemex Tower (1984), the Stock Exchange (1990), and some hotels in the Polanco district. In another context, many wholesale/retail markets were built such as Jamaica, La

Viga, La Merced and La Lagunilla.

One of the projects undertaken during the presidency of Adolfo López Mateos (1958 - 1964) was the construction of the imposing Nonoalco-Tlatelolco complex, with 102 apartment buildings, schools, day nurseries, gardens, clinics and a population of approximately 125,000.

Another stretch of the Anillo Periférico (beltway) was built in the sixties, designed to ease traffic between Lomas de Chapultepec, Ciudad Satélite and the Querétaro highway. Río Churubusco Avenue also dates from this period. The Circuito Interior (inner expressway) and its offshoots were begun in the seventies. Finally, in

Above left. The Museum of Modern Art exhibits outstanding Mexican pictorial works of this century.

Below left. There are "Art Gardens" at different points of the city, where painters display and sell their pictures.

The Rufino Tamayo Museum set in Chapultepec Park houses Mexican and foreign works of art.

the eighties 34 Ejes Viales (arterial avenues) were created covering a total of 113 kilometers in an effort to improve traffic movement.

Work progressed on the Deep Drainage System between 1967 and 1975, which involved the construction of an enormous tunnel to carry the rainwater that accumulated in the metropolitan area through the State of Mexico into Hidalgo.

A few years later, in 1978, an electricity company worker discovered the pre-Hispanic monolith of *Coyolxauhqui* the Aztec Moon goddess. The sculpture, produced between 1480 and 1500 was found at the corner of Seminario and Guatemala streets. The discovery led to the Great Temple project, which was begun with the excavation of 6,000 sq. m. of land. The on-site Museum of

the Great Temple opened its doors in October 1987 to show visitors some remains of Great Tenochtitlan.

Another important museum had opened in 1981: the Rufino Tamayo, built to house the collection of international 20th - century art put together by the great painter during his lifetime. In addition to the permanent display, the museum has organized temporary exhibitions of such important artists as Picasso and David Hockney.

However, the most famous collection in the capital is without any doubt that of the National Museum of Anthropology, built in 1964. This remarkable building houses the most magnificent collection of pre-Hispanic art in Mexico, which ranges from its origins to the masterpieces of Toltec, Olmec, Maya and Aztec sculpture. Pieces such as the *Coatlicue* stone, the Aztec Calendar

Above. The modern National Arts Center located in the south of the city teaches dance, theater, plastic arts and music.

The facade of the Insurgentes Theater is decorated with a mural by Diego Rivera illustrating the "History of the Theater in Mexico".

One of the most picturesque areas in the city is Coyoacán whose etymology —"Place of Coyotes" — was the origin of this lovely fountain on one of the typical squares.

The building for the Centro Mercantil was erected in the late 19th century. This spectacular stained glass dome was designed in 1908 to cover the lobby of what is now a luxurious hotel.

The new Basilica of Our Lady of Guadalupe guards what is the most important image not only for Mexico but for much of Roman Catholic America.

Above right. Groups of dancers often perform at different points in the city, bringing back ancient Aztec splendor with their costumes.

Below right. The architecture on the Square of the Three Cultures in Tlatelolco fuses together three distinct periods: pre-Hispanic, Colonial and Contemporary.

According to tradition the Virgin of Guadalupe appeared to the Indian Juan Diego on Tepeyac hill in 1531. Since then this image, called the Empress of America, has been a symbol of Mexicans' faith.

Mexico is rich in handicrafts, and colorful products from all over the country can be found in the capital.

Above left. One of the most picturesque celebrations in Mexico is the "Day of the Dead" that combines religion, tradition and imagination.

Below left. Death has inspired popular imagination and fantasy in Mexico for a long time. These humorous skulls are on sale in a Mexico City market.

People sometimes need public "scribes" who have used pens, typewriters or rudimentary printing presses to provide their services in the "Portal de Evangelistas" on Santo Domingo Square for many years.

Above left. One of the most striking hand-crafted products is the "charro" hat, part of the typical costume of Mexican countrymen.

Above right. The serape is possibly a hybrid of a native garment, the tilmantli, and the Jeréz shawl of Spain.

Mexico has been famous for its silver deposits ever since colonial times. Nowadays the metal is used to make exquisite necklaces, earrings, bracelets and belt buckles.

"Trees of Life", a popular art form, are made of fired clay and incorporate biblical figures full of naive sincerity.

The pottery known as Talavera or majolica is of fired clay painted with brilliant colors. Although it originates from the city of Puebla, fine examples of this elegant ware with its long tradition can be found in Mexico City.

and part of the priceless treasure from Tomb 7 at Monte Albán in Oaxaca are admired by the hundreds of visitors who arrive every day.

There are also other museums in the city. For example the Museum of Modern Art, the National History Museum in Chapultepec Castle and the Spiral Gallery, the Frida Kahlo, the House and Studio of Diego Rivera, the Anahuacalli, the Children's Museum, also known as Papalote, the Dolores Olmedo, the National Prints Museum, the Museum of Cultures, the Franz Mayer, the National Art Museum and the Palace of Fine Arts Museum, to name a few.

The XIX Olympic Games were held in Mexico City in 1968. This great event gave the city the opportunity to enrich its heritage with large sports facilities - the Sports Palace the Velodrome, the Olympic Swimming pool, the Juan de la Barrera Gymnasium and the Olympic Village with its 24 apartment buildings and various sports and commercial facilities. A Cultural Olympics was held at the same time as the Games. During this event the Paseo

de la Amistad (Friendship Avenue) was opened on the Anillo Periférico, graced by monumental sculptures erected by seventeen artists from five continents.

In September one of the projects that citizens most eagerly awaited was put into full operation: a subway system, generally known as "el Metro".

In late 1970 a new organic law was passed by the Departamento del Distrito Federal (City Government) dividing the area into 16 precincts, namely Alvaro Obregón, Azcapotzalco, Benito Juárez, Coyoacán, Cuajimalpa de Morelos, Cuauhtémoc, Gustavo A. Madero, Miguel Hidalgo, Iztacalco, Iztapalapa, Magdalena Contreras, Milpa Alta, Tláhuac, Tlalpan, Venustiano Carranza and Xochimilco.

Although all of these contain places of historical and tourist interest Xochimilco - "in the place of the fields of flowers" - is one of them that has the longest tradition. Its history goes back to pre-Hispanic times, when it was a village paying tribute to the Aztecs. The original inhabitants were the first to build chinampas to expand their

Mazahua women from the State of Mexico sell their dolls and hand embroideries all over Mexico City.

Mexico's folklore is one of the richest in the world and its dances can be seen in several places in the capital.

Music is also a vital part of Mexico's life today. The world- famous Mariachis are indispensable for enlivening any kind of celebration.

Organ grinders, some of the city's most traditional figures, take us back to the Mexico of yesterday with their old tunes.

The Spanish introduced bullfights into Mexico. The first one in Mexico City on June 24, 1526, was held to commemorate the return of the conquistadors from Honduras.

Above and below right. A bullfight day in the enormous Plaza México, the largest bullring in the world, fills seats and terraces with a colorful noisy crowd of excited fans. Outside there are 26 statues of famous bullfighters and bullfighting scenes, The main entrance shows a picador leading eleven fighting bulls.

Women take an active part in horsemanship displays as can be seen in this spectacular "escaramuza charra".

Right. There are many associations that practice horsemanship in specially built facilities like this one in Mexico City.

The modern horseman in his typical costume continues the tradition of breaking in and handling horses and cattle.

Xochimilco in the south of the city is a favorite place for outings. Its numerous canals banked by flower and vegetable gardens make this locality one of the most pleasant in the city.

Right. Because of its position in the Valley of Mexico, Xochimilco has had plentiful water ever since pre-Hispanic times, and this led to the development of chinampas and an extensive system of waterways.

agricultural lands, long before the Aztecs arrived.
There is also an Olympic sculling canal, built for the 1968 Games, and in 1977 UNESCO designated the zone a World Heritage Site. In the early nineties the city authorities successfully carried out an environmental recovery program in the lake area of Xochimilco. One of the most relaxing trips in the entire city can be taken on a typical *trajinera* (roofed, colorfully decorated flat-bottomed boat) through the canals, past flower-filled chinampas and towering Xochimilco willows, while dozens of herons and ducks fly around.

Another precinct full of old customs and legends is Coyoacán - "Place of coyotes" - in the south of the city. The first Municipal Council was founded here soon after the Conquest. Among the various places of interest are the Frida Kahlo Museum, the National Museum of Popular Cultures and the church of San Juan Bautista on the main square, a typical area that is always alive and bustling.

One of the most outstanding achievements of the seventies was the construction of the new Basilica of Our Lady of Guadalupe, now the resting place of the most important Catholic image in America. There were many reasons for building a new basilica, the main one being that the old one was no longer large enough to receive the countless faithful who arrived every day to prostrate themselves in devotion before the altar.

The Historic Center of Mexico City was created by decree in 1981 when it was decided that special care would be taken of an area that now covers 668 city blocks with 1,436 buildings of historical or architectural interest dating from the 16th to 19th centuries. Like Xochimilco this has been declared a World Heritage Site by UNESCO.

Beginning in the seventies, the city underwent an architectural change. The internationalist ideas of the fifties and sixties began to be left behind since for some they were anachronistic. In the effort to strengthen the new esthetic, buildings were made of concrete - with different finishes - and massive asymmetrical structures arose. The city has notable examples of this architectural trend such as El Colegio de México, opened in 1975, the Centro Cultural

The imagination, sense of humor and ingenuity of Mexicans are reflected every day in even the simplest tasks.

Above left. Mexicans have been great admirers of the country's flora since pre-Hispanic times, and this fondness is the reason for so many stands selling an enormous variety of beautiful sweet-smelling flowers.

Below left. When piñatas, clay pots decorated with paper, are hit and broken with a stick they release a shower of fruit and candies onto the floor. A traditional feature of fiestas and celebrations.

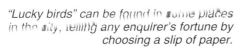

"Lucky birds" can be found in some places in the city, telling any enquirer's fortune by choosing a slip of paper.

Left. Multicolored balloons, cotton candy, delicious fried pastries and amusing pinwheels that spin in the slightest breeze are delights for the eye and palate.

Mexican cuisine, one of the most varied and exotic in the world, is largely based on tortillas, the national staple food. Mexico City has a large number of typical restaurants.

Universitario, on the campus of the National University, and the Head Offices of the Cuauhtémoc Precinct.

In 1982 the city was benefitted by the construction of the Central de Abastos (Central Wholesale Provisions Market) in the Iztapalapa precinct, to which the core of the wholesale trade of the La Merced Market area moved. It has 1,733 storehouses for fruit, vegetables and provisions, together with 770 stands and stores.

In 1985 the President's Office decreed the expropriation of 7,000 buildings and properties in the city center, covering 250 hectares to be used for 50,006 housing units planned and built under the Popular Housing Program. This was a measure recognized internationally by city planners.

Mexico City has approximately 55 radio stations, 9 television channels, nearly 200 public movie theaters, more than 30 newspapers (some of them circulating national-ly), more than 60 museums (which cover all the stages, styles and historical periods that the country has experienced), more than 200 tourist class hotels, over 10 shopping malls and complexes and around 1,000 restaurants for every taste and pocket.

Numerous leisure activities can be enjoyed in agreeable temperatures that usually range fom 20 to 30 degrees Centigrade (68 to 86 degrees Farenheit): soccer matches and football games, bullfights, *charrería* shows (displays of horsemanship), concerts, theater and opera performances, car racing, horse races, and interesting exhibitions in museums and galleries. Both children and adults can have fun in the various amusement parks in the city, especially the one in Chapultepec Park. The list of attractions the city offers is practically endless - just like the imagination of its inhabitants.

MEXICO CITY

Proyect and editorial conception: Casa Editrice Bonechi
Publication Manager: Monica Bonechi
Cover and layout: Sonia Gottardo
Editing: Rita Bianucci

© Copyright by Casa Editrice Bonechi,
Via Cairoli 18b
Tel. +39 55 576841 - Fax +39 55 5000766
E-mail: bonechi@bonechi.it - Internet: www.bonechi.it
50131 Firenze, Italia

ISBN 978-88-8029-632-4

MEXICO CITY

Proyect and editorial conception: Monclem Ediciones
Publication Manager: Concepción Cadena
Cover and layout: Angel Escobar
Editing: Angel Escobar

© Copyright by Monclem Ediciones, S.A. de C.V.
Leibnitz 31
Col. Anzures
11590 México, D.F.-México
Tel. 520 81 67 - Fax 202 88 14

ISBN 968-6434-48-8

Printed in Italy by:
Centro Stampa Editoriale Bonechi

Distribution by:
Monclem Ediciones S.A. de C.V.
Leibnitz 31
Col. Anzures
11590 México, D.F.-México
Tel. 545 77 42
Fax 203 46 57

* · * · *

AUTHOR
Yolanda Bravo Saldaña, a specialist in Mexican art, holds a
degree in Hispanic Language and Literature from the School of
Letters and Philosophy of the Universidad Nacional Autónoma
de México. She holds lectures and writes on this subject.

Translated by: David Castledine

PHOTO CREDITS

G. Dagli Orti, pages: 12 above; 13 above and below; 14; 16
above and below; 17; 18; 19 above and below; 20 belowe; 22
above and below; 23 above and below right; 30; 35 above and
below; 36; 37 above and below; 40; 41 below; 42 above and
below left and right; 43 above and below; 44; 45 above and
below left and right; 46 above and below; 47; 48 above and
below; 49; 50 above; 51 above and below left; 52; 53 above and
below; 54; 55 above; 56; 57 above left and right and below left
and right; 58; 59 above and below; 60 above left and right and
below left and right; 61 above and below; 64; 65 above and
below; 66; 67; 70; 71 above and below; 72 above and below; 74
above and below; 75; 76 above and below; 77 above and below;
78; 79 above and below; 82; 83 above and below; 84 above and below; 85
above and below; 86 above and below; 87 above and below; 88
below; 89; 90 above left and right and below; 91 above and
below; 94; 95 below; 96 above; 97 above; 98 above and below;
102 above; 104; 105; 106 above and below; 107; 108 above; 109
above and below; 110 above; 111 below; 113 above and below;
114 above left and right and below; 115 above left and right; 116
above; 119 below; 122; 125 above and below; 126 above left and
right and below left and right; 127.

Michael Calderwood, pages: 20 above; 21; 23 below left; 38 and
39; 63; 68 and 69; 72 above; 73; 80 and 81; 88 above; 92 and 93;
96 below; 97 below; 99; 100 and 101; 110 above; 111 above;
119 above; 121; 123.

Enrique Franco Torrijos, pages: 6 and 7; 12 below; 15 above left
and right and below left and right; 95 above; 102 below; 103
above and below.

Guillermo Aldana, pages: 112 above and below; 120 above and
below.

Carlos Hahn, pages: 116 below; 117 above; 124 below.

Mónica Castillo Guido, page 124 above.

Martha López, page 108 below.

Monclem Archives, pages: 4; 5; 8; 9 above left and right and
below; 10; 11 above and below; 24; 25; 26 left and right; 27; 28;
29; 30 right; 31; 32; 33 above and below; 34; 41 above; 50
below; 51 below right; 55 below; 62 above and below; 83 above;
110 below; 117 below; 118.

MUSEUMS

• MUSEO NACIONAL DE ANTROPOLOGIA. CIUDAD DE MEXICO.
• MUSEO DEL TEMPLO MAYOR. CIUDAD DE MEXICO.
• MUSEO NACIONAL DE VIRREYNATO. TEPOZOTLAN.
• PINACOTECA VIRREINAL. CIUDAD DE MEXICO.
• MUSEO NACIONAL DE ARTE. CIUDAD DE MEXICO.
• MUSEO DOLORES OLMEDO. XOCHIMILCO. MEXICO, D.F.
• MUSEO DIEGO RIVERA. CIUDAD DE MEXICO.
• MUSEO FRIDA KAHLO.CIUDAD DE MEXICO.
• MUSEO NACIONAL DE HISTORIA. CASTILLO DE CHAPULTEPEC.
  CIUDAD DE MEXICO.